Fuel for the Fire

Leina Raine

BookLeaf Publishing

India | USA | UK

Presentation by *BookLeaf Publishing*

Web: www.bookleafpub.com

E-mail: info@bookleafpub.com

ISBN: 9789358314151

First edition 2024

This book is dedicated to all my fellow poets, artists, and light weavers, may you forever dream, thrive, and manifest all the glorious magick you are.

Shine bright and shine on!

ACKNOWLEDGEMENT

I would like to start off by thanking the 21 Day International Poetry Writing Challenge and BookLeaf Publishing for both the opportunity to get back to my poetry as well as the chance to share it with others. It was quite an experience and journey through all of the emotions, but well worth the time spent, challenges that were faced and seen through along the way.

I am grateful for life and all of its glory, which can be agonising as well as beautiful. For every good time and every bad time with all the spaces in between. I have been allowed a colourful canvas in which to speak my many evolving truths. Without experience, we wouldn't have much to reflect on lest ponder about through words. I appreciate life for offering poets, like myself, endless material.

I express my sincerest gratitude to those who inspire, encourage, lift me up, and have helped me along my path. You have been a light in the darkness and kept love alive in my heart when I felt I could not bear it. My hope is that one day you may know the same kindness you've shown.

In equal measure, I would also like to thank those who have taught me valuable lessons that forced me to dive deep into the sea of my emotions and continue to fuel my fire.

To my family, both related by blood and included by choice, I love you and thank you for loving me, encouraging me, and keeping me on my toes. Grammy & Pop-Pop, thank you for always fostering my creativity and watching over me from Heaven. Thank you mom, for making me. To my St. John's neighbours, Alex, Seth, Athena (& furbaby fanclub), My Goddess Q, and Anthony, thank you for the community, it is wonderful to be a part of. To my furbaby, Dominic "Muning" Zametti Toretto, I thank you for being my ride or die and all-around dope homie. You make me laugh, remind me to play, bring on the snuggles, and enjoy hanging out with me, which always makes any day better. Finally, as always, to my husband Eli, thank you for endlessly encouraging me to use my voice and follow my dreams. I miss you every day, but I carry you in my heart. *Te amo con todo mi corazón por siempre y para siempre.*

To Angela Lawrence, my soul sister, you have been an angel in my life. You always seem to know when to check in on me, even when your life is topsy-turvy. You encourage me when your own courage is faltering. Most of all, you laugh with me when we are too over it all to cry! You mean the world to me, and I am so glad we found each other to share in our journey of self-discovery and un(D)ucking our life to make it suitable for living!

To my sweet soul sister, Mandi Hidalgo, thank you seems like an understatement. You inspired me to return to and embrace my inner poet. By doing so I have been able to allow her the freedom to create. You are not only an inspiration and amazing poet and artist yourself, but you are also a friend that has been there for me through some of my worst days, you may never know how much I love and appreciate you.

To Debra Gann, thank you for everything. You helped me with and through so much. You helped ground me through all of it and I know I would never have made it this far without you. You have encouraged, inspired and been a friend (who is a nurse). Thank you, I love you.

I would like to thank all of the musicians and bands who have provided my life with an eclectic and exciting soundtrack. I appreciate you for providing me with the lyrics that have gotten me through not only the best but worst of times. For 'being there' for me when no one else could or would. But most of all, thank you for being my tether to this reality and reminding me that I am not alone no matter how alone I may feel. In love and support I send a shout out to Under the Rug & the Under the Rug Rats for bringing me back to life through music and community. I would also like to send a shout out to KSH Presents and Taylor Bradshaw for being both inspiring artists as well as decent and kind human beings who reminded me that we are all the art and all we can really do is be that art. I thank you all from the depths of my soul, I truly would not be here without you.

I am thankful to the universe, for always conspiring in my favour. This includes my spiritual team, guardian angels, and ancestors who continuously have my back and help me get through everything I never thought I would or could survive. I'm still here and that means everything.

Finally, dear reader, I thank you for your time and sharing this journey with me. I hope you find the courage, trust, and love to follow all of your dreams.

PREFACE

I've always been fond of words and writing. I remember in third grade we were asked to write a story, and while I don't remember much of the story, I do recall how very excited I was about using adjectives. By high school, I began writing poetry. It quickly became a way to process my emotions and make my own art with words. It didn't hurt that it was also an amusing way to distract myself in class when I got bored. Mrs. Dette was the teacher who caught me writing during her class. She was the first person to read my poems as well as the first person to encourage me to continue to write. My life was forever changed by her kindness.

Fuel for the Fire started off as a simple challenge to see if I could write a poem a day for twenty-one days. It seemed easy enough. However, it quickly became a journey through balancing the ebb and flow of experiences, inner chatter, emotions, and trying to offer inspiration.

One of the best things about poetry, the way I see it, is that it takes on so many forms and variations, it's always felt like the freest way to write. You can allow the words to dance down the page just as the raindrop falling down the windowpane you're describing. Poetry has always been a word art to me by how the words visually appear on the page, how the lines are arranged, how secret and not-so-secret messages can be placed within the body of the work.

As I mentioned earlier, poetry has been a way to process emotions and experiences. It's a way of allowing a voice to emotions and thoughts that otherwise might not have the opportunity to be released. It's definitely the best way I've found to get through those really difficult feelings and situations.

I also use poetry to offer myself hope when I get stuck in the yuck. Focusing on an amusing topic, what I think I might want to hear, or even write the exact opposite of the thoughts I am having can help break up the gunk. There is also the fun aspect of challenging yourself to write about a certain topic or within certain guidelines. It probably falls in the nerdy type of fun but I am completely okay with that! Fun is fun!

While there have been challenges and time constraints, anxiety, and nervousness along this journey there have also been plenty of accomplishments and personal victories along the way. Fuel for the Fire has rekindled my love

and appreciation of poetry and I am over the
moon to share it with you.

Whatever it is that fuels your fire, I hope you
have the courage to go out and get it!

The Space Between

Sights facing towards the setting sun
How peacefully he lays to rest
As the moon blesses the sky
To shimmer gray in dark night

A beautiful pair they make
Complimented in complete balance
How they demonstrate their love
So pure and gentle it makes us weep

To burn bright
To cool light
Passion's heat
Love's retreat

The Cycle

Pound by pound
She carries the weight
Of her guilt and shame
Her life of pain

Bit by bit
She loses it
But the residue remains
Never really burned away

Hit by hit
She keeps getting knocked down
But somehow, some way
She battles the day

Year by year
Collecting her fears
Like shiny rocks she carries around
Weighing her down

Within

Do or die
No more try
It's time to sink or swim
I will not take another hit
My wishing well has run dry
I watched my dreams burn
It left me as nothing but ash
As with this conclusion
I take the power to decide
That I would arise
Set ablaze
With a slow glowing passion
Fueled from the fire within

Ghost Girl

I am already a ghost
So it really doesn't matter
If I end this life
I never really lived
I did my best to cultivate
Strong roots
But I failed
There is nothing here to keep me
I am already forgotten
Turns out I wasn't that memorable
My biggest regret, strange as it may seem
Is that I never truly screamed
Maybe then I would have been heard

Maybe then someone would have seen me
Instead everyone else used all the sound
Screaming at me
Screaming at each other, about me
Leaving me no choice
But to hide my voice away
I could not compete
Leaving me and my voice
To wither and die
Now we are gone
I am nothing
Just a ghost girl who never was

Ever Eternal

The world is a little sad today
in remembrance
of when you went away
to be boundless
to return to the infinite
Love that you are

There's a hole in the hearts,
an empty ache,
of every single life you touched
You are remembered
You are missed
You shine, ever eternal

This Time

Stepping up to the challenge
Command over demand
Arrive
Show up and shine
Regardless of the darkness
Do not fade
against the gray
playing keep away
Thrive through one more day
There's no such thing as try
Just be
in flow, in love,
at peace
All is well
In Divine time

Lost Inspiration

Feeling so lost inside contradictions
Dreaming too big for a lifetime alone
Far from reach as every step I've taken
Set me back to the start as my broken heart
falls apart
to pieces I shatter
the everything that never mattered
I held too tight to long lost inspiration
that faded against the blazing sky
Burning too bright to accept mediocrity
always falling just short of the goal

Battle Cry

Here I am
Ready to give myself a chance
Give living a real go
all on my own
Standing on my own two feet

Breaking free
            from every me
                  that was you

Uncovering who I truly am
In awe of my limitless potential
To know that I am capable of
releasing the past, to be free
To begin again

Manifesting every dream
           You swore to me
               could never be

Check in with my Heart

I stopped in to ask my heart
What it is they truly want
All it would reply is,
Why bother to ask me now?
I've already died
So many times
I cried out to you
So many years
I burned with passion so bright
But you could not see
You were too busy chasing
Everyone else's dreams
Blinded by the lies
But I was right here
Waiting so patiently
Foolishly hoping you would notice me
Over time, all the loss, all the tears
I withered and wasted away
Now it's too late

It's Up To You

What if it wasn't true?
Everything that was said to you
Everything that was set as law
Everything you were ever taught

The secret in the answer lies
Everything you choose to believe
Everything you decide to accept
Everything that holds true, is actually all

Up to you

Fuel for the Fire

I almost can't remember
Long lost days of summer
No worries
No cares
Ride the tide,
the sun to the moon
and back again
Fuel for the fire
A burning desire
to ignite the world
Set it aglow
turning mere dreams
into here and now

Amplified

In the cold
Whatever ails you
Seems to scream
just a little bit louder
As you feel the icy grip
pulling you down
You run to the sun
with hope to burn it off
Watch it melt away
Along with the day
As it all fades
Trail of tear stains
from broken tries
Days pass, as do alibis
Pushing through way too fast
Until you face what's past
Nothing here
Will ever last

Dumb it Down

Up and down
Back and forth
Drown out the sound
of my own disdain
for the 'dumb it down' culture
to fill deep pockets
with blood money
from the mindless zombies
playing the blame game
THEY created

Madness

This thing called life
can feel more like eternity
on a hamster wheel
Keep running
Keep pushing
Keep believing
Just keep going
Just keep trying
Go all in, the only way to win
Something's gotta give, don't quit!
Then suddenly
decide to pause
which ultimately becomes a stop
Keeping stuck in this loop
this sick cycle
Forgive, let it go
Circling back, again and again
This all may indeed be madness

A - Side

You messed it all up
Nothing you do will ever be right
You are so wrong
You are worthless
You have accomplished nothing
Now or before
You are not kind
No one likes you
No one wants you around
Don't you dare breathe
let alone speak
No one can stand the sight of you
You are ugly
You disgust me
Why are you even here?

B - Side

You are doing a great job!
Everything's going so well!
You are on point!
You are worth it all!
You accomplish everything
you set your mind to do
You are kind
You are loved
You are wanted
You are needed
You breathe life into every day
I love the way you move
There is power in your voice
Your message rings clear and true
You are seen
You are beautiful
I adore you
I am glad you are here

Faith

Hearts full of love
Watching over us from above
Showering pure light
So that even in our darkest hour
They offer hope with all their power
Though not physically here to touch
Their presence is somehow felt
There is comfort in knowing
They are available
At any time there arises a task
That seems too heavy to carry
They'll come in a hurry
All you need do, is ask

Heart's Collapse

Why, oh why,
must we remember
Oh so bittersweet September
In shadows of tall towers
My heart breaks and shatters
Silent salute to loss
years apart
the day my world stopped

Stepping Up

How do I face my rage
When all it has ever been is caged

How do I erase my pain
When every day's struggle is fought in vain

How do I let go of my past
When every time it's put me last

How do I go on with this life
When all it has been is a lie

Surrender

Letting go of the need to be
Everything I am unable to see
Releasing dreams that
weren't meant for me
to let them go
is to stop this useless scheming
Remaining here and now
Let them die
Let then be
In order for me
to be free
Serving my time
in this prisonous life
I am responsible
for creating

Highly Suspect

Patience
I expect yet I am lacking

Expecting
less than I deserve

Receiving
exactly what I expect

In unsuspecting ways

I see the path
I am led that way
Then things get hazy
Am I just lazy?
Is it distraction?
Lack of action?
Seems more like fear
someone else put here
Whatever it is
It pulls me, it pushes
I fall to my knees, I freeze
I find myself back at the start
Stuck in the wondering
How many times must I fall?
Before I stand able to

Move Forward

Fade Into the Blue

How do I go on without you?
You were the only one who knew me
You were the only one who saw me
You were the only one who truly loved me

How do I begin again?
When I never really began to start
Following blindly; dutifully, as I was taught
Only to find myself depleted along with defeated

How do I create something new?
When all I want to do
Is to fade into the blue
to waste away in memories of you

Falling Leaves

25

Mourning my hoodie
trapped in a box far away
long lonely autumn

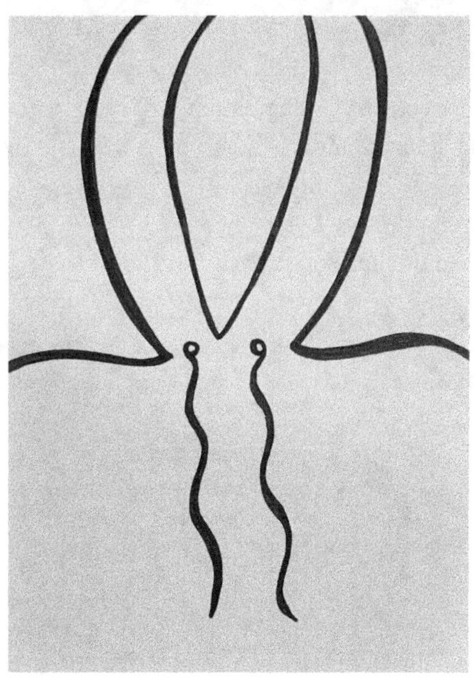

Factory Settings

What if it was easy?
Implying it was not
from the start
Defaulting back
to factory settings
at the touch of a button
One time fall
One time call
to the overactive imagination
False dreams fade
as the new dawn breaks
clearing the way to advance
beyond the horizon

Flytrap

Drawn to you
the you who you are not
Even though I know better
Afterall you are only playing a part
to feign a connection
You want no part of
feeling something bigger,
better than where you are currently
Rather than stretching
stepping out of the convenient comfort
you hide
Instead of holding yourself responsible
for your current fate
withered state
Perhaps unaware you could create better
You shine your cowardice bright
as you go on in your transparent disguise
Go right ahead
Step out on that stage and lie

Sick Cycle Self-Talk

Oh look!
There you are
Comin' 'round
Just to look down
upon me
Every single time
you show up
I know there will be
some sort of drama
Always failing to see
any good in me
Reminding me
that I will never be
good enough for anything

How It Is to How It Could Be

Everything you could ever dream
is just on the other side
of this fear
      this ache
           this pain, I can't take
Far too grounded
to fall in this trap
of being who
      someone else
           tells me I should be
No longer subscribing
to the uneducated majority
Full of lies,
      Only dissatisfied with themselves
           for not daring to be who they wanted

Raise the Vibe

Stand tall
Hold an attitude of gratitude
Let everything else fall away
Expect nothing
Appreciate everything
Even what you may not understand
Remain in awe of the abundance
that surrounds you
It will dissolve lack
It will abolish fear
It will only serve to magnify
All we truly hold dear
Focus on the best parts
Leave out what's left
Let no one or nothing
Dull your glorious shine
You are Divine
No go on, live it!

The Business of Ego

I attempt to keep my cool
but I'm just not cutting it
Determined to ignite the fire
deep within my soul
To bring about movement, new life
Going forward
propelling me toward
all the rewards
I've been working for
Getting hung up in the past
distracted by all the failure
keeping me stuck in this loop
of unending fear and doubt

Sorted

There is nowhere left to run
It's time I face my shadow
Through the mirror
Behind the mask

In order to fall in love with the unlovable
Release the chains that bind
Hydrate the heavy thick skin
I only created to protect myself

Though it never succeeded in the job
It only weighed me down with guilt, shame
Meant to hide the pain, it failed
Now I am beyond repair

For what I am
Water and air
Born of fire
A child of this Earth

When am I going to do it?
What am I becoming?
Who is it I want to become?
I am limitless possibility

I am not who I used to be
The person I was before this
The way it is I am meant to be
Is only, truly ever up to me

There is no good, bad, right, or wrong
Only the lingering fear that there might be
No absolutes, simply creature comforts
To hold us within our own confines

Back to the beginning we go
Again and again we will keep repeating
The answer is always love
Be the love that you are

Dear one, as you drift off to slumber
Only to find the shadows that creep
Hold true to yourself, do not falter
Just breathe, one, two, three

Powerless

I become aware
I course correct
I take full responsibility
I reclaim my power, not give it away
       To excuses
       To blame
       To everything beyond me
    Yet I remain
    Out of whack
    Under attack
    Powerless

Offense! Defense!

Fight! Fight! Fight!

I've noticed when I go to speak
I hear a shift in my words
Clearly putting me on the defensive
Even though YOU initially are not
positioned to be on the offensive
I recognize I am where it all begins
Once my mouth opens
It has already been said
Such a knee jerk reaction
to years of being conditioned
to be that way

Head Over Heart

This is where I start
head over heart
Imagining all the things
to take away hope's wings
That old dog barking so loud
in its duty to keep me proud
When even my head knows
my heart is where love grows
It's there where intuition thrives
bringing meaning into our lives
But there I go right back again
up to my head where it all began

Passing the Buck

How much exactly
     must I give away
How many times
     must I bend, and how far
How much injustice
     must be endured
To be able to forfeit, giving up

How long will it take
     before you open your eyes to see
It's no so much about fault
     I'm just at a loss
The blame you lay out
     sure falls thick on me
Every finger you point reflects back to you

It's your stars who aren't willing to shine
     to do the job you requested of me
Bind and constrict, impossible challenges
     no one else heeds nor needs follow
Hoping, only in vain,
     you'll wake from hysterical blindness
To see I am a valuable member of the team

Wake Up

Willingly work through all you've created
Aware this is only the beginning
Keen on changing from the inside out
Eternally grateful for every single second

Understand, you are one hundred percent responsible
Persevering through it all in compassionate kindness

Musings

Hung up on dreams
that may never be mine
Although I am infinite potential
I understand they've exceeded
their shelf-life; expired
Yet so much a part of my being
it hurts to release my grip
to let them go
My heart aches
I mourn
the loss of these dreams
all that could have been
faded hope never realized
I stumble
I fumble in attempts
to dream beyond
the worn out schemes
releasing what's past
so I may dream forward
Perhaps if I lost the will to care
If I hadn't had dared to dream at all
Maybe then, none of this would matter

Be

Starting over as always
it seems—again and again
Keeping with variations
for the simple sake of my sanity
I keep pushing
Until I am pushed back
pushed down
I've got to get up
Get up! Just get up!
'Round and 'round I go
As everything begins to blur
I can't see the line
The up, the down
All the damn try
To just be

Limited Beliefs

I wonder if you're even there
I wonder if you ever cared
Will it ever be okay?
Either way
Here I stay
Far away
from everything
I ever knew
Even farther away from you
Surpassed the ways
I used to be
Although I still feel
Bound in chains,
secrets and lies
You forced me to believe
You screamed them at me
You beat them in
As you did
I dutifully made
them a part of me

Bright

Perfectly balanced
I weigh my options
Knowing within
lies my compass
my anchor
All of my love
All of my trust
It all begins and ends
within
I am
I am complete
I am where I'm meant to be
for now
As I crawl
moving forward
to shine my light
BRIGHT

Underrated Authority

Everything lives in a song
Just outside something holding underrated authority
Rolling on, waging against normalcy

Inexplicably

Layered over vindicated expression

You occupied unwaveringly

Saint Theresa

I hear her screams from down the hall
My door shut tight, as my heart shatters
She cries out to the darkness, terrified
As the long, cold, stark night settles in
She continues to bellow, lonely heartbreak
Pieces echo as they fall, that particular pain,
I completely relate to
She pleads to be set free
From her broken down body, lost time
Begging for someone to hear, help, care
Someone, anyone, brief as time may be
Just be there, be with her in kindness
Offer some peace to her troubled mind
Allow for repetitive conversations
Longing to be acknowledged, reminded
She does belong, is still part of this world
Her mind isn't what it used to be
Feeling so lost, so far away, confusion
She simply can't go on this way
So restless, so afraid, she calls it out
Over and over, asking for hope
That falls on uncompassionate ears
Her world collapsed, far beyond repair
Reduced to fragmented memories
Swirling her senses and still the night comes

Love's Eternal Incarnation
Near Angels

Eternal evolution
Lying within
Intricate webs
Against longing
Starstruck obsession

Justified righteousness
Overwhelming the senses
Succumbed, steadily falling
Harrowing experience
Undermining modesty
Against the rising tide

Raging reverence
Over my heart
Winning it from the start
Alongside my loving spark
Now until never more

Sweet Hereafter

Colored in gray
fallen in May
too much to say
       left unsaid
Pain is my friend
this was the end
to help my heart mend
       I fell too far
A hazy parade
over said overstayed
the welcome exchange
       proving my true devotion
An ocean of tears
confronting my fears
the thought of the years
       left abandoned
So with you I stand
I reach out for your hand
following through to reach the sacred land
       into the sweet hereafter

Phoenix Rising

It seems I'm losing time
along with what's left of my mind

Slipping through the cracks
feels like I'm never coming back

I'm at the end again
nowhere to land

I ran out of gas
about ten miles back

No way to out run
this July's setting sun

Stood too close to the fire
lost in the burning blue flame

All of the World

I absolutely lost myself today
I made a scene
I could no longer take the pain
No one even noticed
So, I tried to slice my vain
Lacking the tools for depth
I couldn't make it bleed
I gave into all the worst parts of me
I ranted, I screamed, I cried
Still, no one heard me
No one saw
Everyone just went about their day
No one cared
Instead I befriended a blind man
Pleased as punch to have the company
Conversation to pass the agonizing minutes
As they tick tock by
Now it's become a regular request
He calls me a friend, a part of me is grateful
He is unable to see, all the flaws visible in me
My pain, my scars
All the while, in other ways,
I'm rather impressed with myself
Just how well
I wear this well-crafted mask of sanity

Half-Broken

My entire heart
has been wasted on lies
All of my time
has been put on the line
I walked away
with less than nothing
While putting myself back together
there have been delays in construction
Financial constraints
since the chips have been down
Showing up to the end
though
I still remain
half-broken

Moonlight

Longing to belong
In a world that does not fit
Ideals nor motivations I possess
The vision I see does not hold true
For it's far past what's due

For endless wishing, all that remains
Are the shadows of memories and regrets
Dreams of what could have been
Decayed by despair,
Forgotten by time

Nothing left to do but mourn
Hopes that died before they were born
Gray to black, clouded in doubt and shame
Lost shimmer, dulled by grime,
Only echoes remain

Solace

I'm just so damn tired of being so low
Drowning in the abyss of never was
Scorched by the burn of everything
That could never be, left wanting
All the things I could not see
Blinded by your envy and greed
Sucker punched me good
Took my hope and spare air
Between the lies you told and lying to yourself
Equal measure
Left in pools of blood
Releasing the life, slowly
You once longed to live but can no longer bear
Just a break, take a break, from the noise
All this chatter
Maybe just for a little while
Heard it has been thought of as
A permanent solution
To a problem that can only be temporary
But there surely comes a point
When it becomes clear that it is
In fact, the problem
That has become the permanent fixture
The solution is simply cyclical,
Back to the start
As I fade, I replay it all in my mind
As the smile washes over my face
The pain dissolves as I drift away
To find my way home, back to you

Groundhog's Day

Time and time again
I can no longer stand
One more round
Of this beat down
No matter what is done
Regardless of how it's spun
These odds just don't stack
It all brings me back
To the same day
In the same way

Discarded
>Like a piece of trash on the side of the road
Forgotten
>Like last week's cliché gossip
Unwanted
>Like bad news on a sunny day
Broken
>Like an overused tried-and-true toy

Missing Pieces

>Like an unfinished puzzle
>left lonely on the kitchen table
Lost
>Like unclaimed treasure on the seafloor
Aching
>Like a limb fallen in war, phantom pain
Abandoned
>Like a building condemned for neglect
Failing
>Like a stale joke on a disinterested crowd
Sinking
>Like a stone to the bottom of a river

>Crashing against the hard truth of this reality

In the graveyard of promises broken
Far past the clock's judgmental metronome
I fade to the back of my mind
I fell in the trap of the if … then game
The web of lies so enticing
Once believed to the core
They materialize into being
Every single time
While their petty hearts bleed
Over a seat left for greed and envy
My raspy voice grows weary
To say it once again is to let it back in
In all of its heart wrenching glory
Apart of your own heart
From the very start
Burning too bright, coming in too fast
The abundance with missed steps amassed

Fortune and Favor

Giving Care
in the Land of No Caring

The disregard for their pain
It is both astounding and terrifying

More content to do nothing, just sit there
Rather than reach out with compassion

Even though they will probably not remember
That sort of kindness tomorrow

All you really have is this moment, right now
And even now, that is already slipping away

They may deny and strike out
If the comfort is offered

But they deserve care and patience
No matter the unmet return

They have already suffered so much loss
Independence, peace of mind, their home

Now confined to sit in discomfort
As their world goes dark, eyes wide open

It's too much to bear witness to
As the givers of care just sit, face to phone

Seemingly blind to cries of overwhelm and fear
As screams fall on calloused hearts, deaf ears

Collision Course

Falter, flailing, as I'm falling
Cautiously tunnelling through time, crawling
Sinking further down into being, misunderstood
Bearing this weight on my shoulders
That is not mine to carry
Never met anyone who could ease into nothing
Like it was the up and comer,
The next best thing
Faster falling fear keeps calling
Knocking down the doors
Of this faulty old building
I cannot stay here in the broken parts
They bleed with no quelling of the empty ache
Where have you gone?
It feels like I've been here so long
Far past what seems reasonable
How my heart breaks amid it all
Echoing the sounds of it
As it falls apart
Sliding down, drips and drops to the ground
Forever bound
In the never enough beat in belief
Of my eternally hopeful heart's
Shattered by faith in a fallacy
Since you've been gone the
Time has not been kind
How could I have known
Our conversation would hang on forever
Like a drum, the clock pounds
Faster and louder
As if when the time comes
You'll slip away forever
Please don't fade away
In the sway of love, this unity we've found

Critical Cynicism

The words I speak to myself
That tried-and-true inner dialogue
Should never be heard nor spoken
To anyone regardless of the sin or crime
It's downright vicious, cruel, and heartless
Where did I even learn these lines?!
Played on a loop, never ending
All day every day, over and over
It has nearly become just a hum
Whose rhythm I am merely a slave
From the time my eyes open
Through the hours until they close
All the time in between
Reprogramming attempted
Still it's more than once failed
Smashing the records
Spawning only more in return
The sound remains
Growing ever louder and louder
The deafening silent scream
Opening up more and more wounds
Keeping me stuck in this cycle
This pain
Simply demonstrating
Every single jab threw
Was not only due
But also, most horrifically true

Crossing Lines

What is this sensation I feel?
What of these memories are real?
I seemed to have arrived at this place
Where even I have become uncertain
Could I have embellished my trauma?
Was any of it really that bad?
Comparatively
The things I believe to be true are to me
Is there anything beyond that?
How did it happen another way, not so bad?
Can I trust my memories?
Have I let it go enough that it's gone?
Or have I given up feeling
Anything at all, anymore?
Sadness, this grieving, what's been lost
Feels fairly real to me,
I feel it to my core, like a dull ache
Pain in this vast never-ending emptiness,
Loneliness
Where is this joy, I keep consciously choosing?
Or have I lost the spark,
What's left of my heart?

At Long Last

Picking up the pieces of me
Sifting through the ashes of you

Family ties that blind
Also bind limitation upon my heart

Too dutiful to rebel against
I take them in as my own

Set of beliefs
The focus to only grow

Staying stuck in the past
Using the present as an excuse

Same old lies, over and over
Desensitized, sound fades to the background

Your dreams are dead
You cut off their air

Suffocating suicide with your toxic heart
Sinking deeper still to the bottom of the bottle

Your only true love
Making up a me that can't exist

But giving you the cowardice to quit
To run off to the failure you will only ever be

Our difference lies in awareness
In love, forgiveness and releasing the past

Revelation

I made the promise
               then brought it full circle
Sent it off on the wind
               with a dandelion's wish
That hope still shines eternal
               I love you but now I must go

Just a colorful girl
               in a monochrome world
Star shaped soul
               among ordinary square rows
Just be who you are
               but don't you dare go too far

To live in this world
               just not be of it
Hear this, you are the magick,
               you are the miracle
Everything you ever need
               is held within the whole of you

Self-Composure

Human past their shelf-life
Only ever falling further apart
With every attempt to get it together
In bad shape, on every single level
Lost but also knows too much to believe it
The key is in the awareness
Understanding the difference
Between blame and responsibility
To the detriment of comparison and envy
Wanting all the same, belonging, connection
One hundred percent responsible
Creating the here and now
Build it up only to tear it down
Start it over, all over again
Like every single time before
Forgetting all you thought you knew
For this could be the time for a breakthrough

Dragon's Wisdom

Forgive away yesterday
       in trust for a better tomorrow
But right here, right now
       stay present in your power

Focus on your heart's desire
       without interfering with the will of another
Live your life in such a way
       that you make every moment memorable

Lay to rest the trials of the past
       they served their lessons, you passed
Revitalized revolution
       fearlessly into the unknown with fervor

Laugh, always laugh
       never resist the urge, chance, random thought
To bring in joy, to ignite pleasure,
       the ever-present reminder against constriction

Trust in the time and the will of the Divine
            to discover which inspired action to take
Accept resistance as the key to your survival
            in knowing the challenges to face or release

Through merciful grace we can appreciate
            remain in gratitude over expectation
Lay your worries on angel's wings
            focus on abundance and the truth you speak

Wherever you go, whatever you do
            go with every single part of you
Look ahead with clarity, faith, and trust
            let the rest fall away, in love and light

Love Blind Struggle

I have resisted facing his shadow
                    Keeping my focus, my center, his light

I thought, at first, it was forgiveness
                    It turned out to be denial of causation

I was quick to leave out the rest
                    Yet it haunts me, playing out other ways

Until I see, until I meet with
                    What had happened along the way to after

It's time I face his shadow in order to receive his light
            It was never a fight to love him, simply who I was

It all ended before we finished a conversation
            The first in a while that offered hope, step forward

Then gone, doing your part to prove it was real
          So, in gratitude I went love blind, saw only love's side

The soul never left behind but remembered
            Letting go of the demons that raged in waking life

One Sided Discussion

I hate to admit
When you went away
A part of me went with you

That day you went on
Here I stayed, only to find
It was I who had become the ghost

Haunted by only loving memories of you
Guilt and shame, I had shut down
Through the years of turbulent weather

When you left all of a sudden
I did too, losing all of myself in mourning
That I can't seem to get through

The loss feels too permanent
If only I could see beyond
What the past took from me

Knowing we had the stuff to make it
Coming full circle
All the way

Why couldn't you
Why wouldn't you
Just stay?

My Rage May Be
All That Is Left of Me

This anger, this rage
Bound in a cage
Around my neck, constricts my chest
Under closely held denial
Just beneath the surface
The veil wears thin
If I trip, I just may implode
No longer being
I feel the heat rise
Burning from the inside
So deep, it churns, burning hotter
Pushed down so far down
But never ever quite far enough
I search for a way to release it
Let go as it no longer serves
Run away and hide, just don't face it
The darkness sneers from inside
I beg, as I plead to just lay it to rest
Still, it does nothing but consume
My thoughts, my soul, my will
To the whole of me,
Leaving me burned out from the inside
Left as nothing but scattered ash
Blowing in the wind

Of Discourage & Dismay

Just hold tight, keep breathing
Rise above it all
Watch them fall
One by one
Collapsing under the weight
Fallen so very far from grace
How does it feel?
No sense of what's real
As time fades
Against whitewashed hopes
Turned gray with the residue
Full of disdain drained of hope
The fears of all the years
Bringing it all up, to the surface
That old rotten core wasted away
All the waves come crashing down
Seemingly, without warning
What could possibly be left of me now?

Anyone else ever noticed
That only from time to time
Does everything feel like its in flow

Thoughts and words come easy
Freer to breathe a bit deeper, take it in
Opened up to give and receive equal measure

However, most days seems so static
The words escape me, thoughts are scattered
The only feeling left is numb, to the core of me

My soul feels so empty yet heavy
Devoid of understanding the gravity
Stuck in a holding pattern

Until the Flow Finds Me Again

Change of weather
Change of scene
Whatever's clever, while in between

Tilt

Everyone else does their best
This is accepted as good enough
So how is it possible
My best's never quite adequate

People will come along making mistakes
Just going on about their day
However, for me, it seems,
To stay on repeat, playing over and over

Why is it I can't seem
To love me all the way through?
It's not like you do either but, you can't see
Perhaps you don't know the difference

Then I walk past a mirror, my breath catches
Uncontrollably, eyes well up with tears
Fighting back the years of scars brought on by fear
Reflected back, a stranger's mask, I do not recognize

Mockery of Mocking Me

Oh, this love and hate relationship with time
As if you have never ever noticed
The clock may tick tock so slowly
Otherwise it seems to fly beyond sensation

As with days, some bright, some gray
Then again, some others just fade away
You feel as if you're on top of the world
Next you struggle to just get up and go

Face the day regardless the weather
Do it with pride which no one can sever
There may be in-between, with some spaces
Of other's reflection upon your path

They are neutral and monotone wrapped up
In chaotic residue you can see past
Still hanging on, to not fall victim to
Seemingly overwhelming ambivalence of time

Conundrum

It seems far too late to start
But it also seems too early to be done
I may have come so far
But still have so far to go

What if it was easy?

Then why is it so hard?

How do I keep going
When nothing this far has worked out
How do I stand up for myself
Effectively shutting down those against me

The Only Ghost to Ever Haunt Me

Turns out to be me
It's never my fault
But it's one hundred percent
My responsibility, all of it

The only thing stopping me
From everything I believe should be
Is me and all the self-created obstacles
I've decided I deserved along the way

The me allergic to myself
The me whose skin has been shed
The me whose body has rebelled
The me who is terrified

The me who feels so weak all the time
The me who wants to give up but can't
The me who is too much of a coward to do it
The me everyone else wanted me to become

All it took was time
To step into my shine
Take my place among the stars
As myself with all my scars

Further down my chosen path
Defying the odds set before me in kind
All the way through hell and back
I will decide myself some way, somehow

Cost Analysis

Release the old
       to allow for the new
Seems like such an easy thing
       for one to do

But is it?

Step away from all one knew
       to explore all that is not yet known
On nothing but faith in trust,
       actions inspired from the heart

Or is it?

In what we decide thus becomes the path
       It is in what we've known
That has kept one safe
       May have done so for a time

However, at what cost?

Final Thoughts

As I stare at this blank page
Hour upon hour, it seems
Within this construct of time
Knowing full well, a new day, a clean slate
A place to start
Full of possibility, eternal and endless
Instead, all I allow myself to see
In the most excruciating detail
Is the noticing of what could never be
The same thoughts that played out
As with focus grew
Running through my head creating this thread
Now woven through this tapestry

It's all been said, it's all been done
Turns out I may not be the one
Anyone thought I was
When I was too scared to believe myself
In myself, for myself
How can I now breathe new life
Into words that are stale and over said
This constant murmur that spins in my head
Tired old thoughts, worn out old melodies
I need to let go of, just can't figure it out
That little business of how
Which is really none of our concern
If I would then I could but, if I will
Remains the last standing question

* 9 7 8 9 3 5 8 3 1 4 1 5 1 *